IPHIGENIA CRASH LAND FALLS ON THE NEON SHELL THAT WAS ONCE HER HEART

(A rave fable)
inspired by Euripides'
IPHIGENIA AT AULIS

Caridad Svich

BROADWAY PLAY PUBLISHING INC
224 E 62nd St, NY, NY 10065
www.broadwayplaypub.com
info@broadwayplaypub.com

First printing: November 2012
Seconding printing: August 2013
I S B N: 978-0-88145-541-0

Book design: Marie Donovan
Page make-up: Adobe Indesign
Typeface: Palatino
Printed and bound in the U S A

CONTENTS

ABOUT THE AUTHOR

Caridad Svich is a U S Latina playwright, translator, lyricist and editor whose works have been presented across the U S and abroad at diverse venues, including Borderlands Theater, Denver Center Theatre, Cincinnati Playhouse in the Park, Gala Hispanic Theatre, Repertorio Espanol, 59East59, McCarren Park Pool, Miracle Theatre, Mixed Blood Theatre, Repertorio Espanol, 7 Stages, Salvage Vanguard Theatre, Teatro Mori (Santiago, Chile), ARTheater (Cologne), and Edinburgh Fringe Festival/U K. She received a 2012 OBIE Award for Lifetime Achievement in the theatre, and the 2011 American Theatre Critics Association Primus Prize for her play The House of the Spirits, based on the novel by Isabel Allende. She has been short-listed for the PEN Award in Drama three times, including in the year 2010 for her play Instructions for Breathing. Among her key works: 12 OPHELIAS (a play with broken songs), ALCHEMY OF DESIRE/ DEAD-MAN'S BLUES, ANY PLACE BUT HERE, IPHIGENIA CRASH LAND FALLS ON THE NEON SHELL THAT WAS ONCE HER HEART (a rave fable), FUGITIVE PIECES, GUAPA, IN THE TIME OF THE BUTTERFLIES (based on the novel by Julia Alvarez), Love in the Time of Cholera, (based on the novel by Gabriel Garcia Marquez), THE WAY OF WATER, THE TROPIC OF X and the multimedia collaboration The Booth Variations.

She has been profiled in *American Theatre* and The *Huffington Post,* among others. She has edited several books on theater including *Out of Silence: Censorship in Theatre & Performance* (Eyecorner Press), *Trans-Global Readings and Theatre in Crisis?* (both for Manchester University Press) and *Divine Fire* (BackStage Books). She has translated nearly all of Federico Garcia Lorca's plays and also dramatic works by Julio Cortazar, Lope de Vega, Calderon de la Barca, Antonio Buero Vallejo and contemporary plays from Mexico, Cuba and Catalonia. Among her awards: a Radcliffe Institute for Advanced Study Fellowship at Harvard University, a T C G/Pew National Theatre Artist Residency, an N E A/T C G Fellowship, Thurber House Fellowship, the HOLA Award for Outstanding Achievement in Playwriting, the Whitfield Cook Award for New Writing from New Dramatists, the Rosenthal New Play Prize, and the 2009 Lee Reynolds Award from the League of Professional Theatre Women awarded annually to a distinguished female artist for their commitment to social and political change in the arts.

She is alumna playwright of New Dramatists, founder of NoPassport theatre alliance & press (http://www. nopassport.org), Drama Editor of *Asymptote* journal of literary translation, associate editor of Routledge/U K's *Contemporary Theatre Review* and contributing editor of TheatreForum. She holds an M F A in Theatre-Playwriting from U C S D, and has taught creative writing and playwriting at Bard College, Barnard College, Bennington College, Ohio State University, Rutgers University-New Brunswick, and Yale School of Drama. She is an entry in the Oxford Encyclopedia of Latino Literature. Website: www.caridadsvich.com

Juárez's Dead Girls:
De-romanticizing feminicidio in Caridad Svich's IPHIGENIA...A RAVE FABLE
Amy Littlefield

In the lead sentence of a 2009 article about the murders of hundreds of young women in the Mexican border city of Juárez, one Los Angeles Times reporter wrote: "The streets of Juarez are swallowing the young and pretty."

This dramatic lead, like much of the writing done about the rapes and murders of women in Juárez, romanticizes the crime by drawing attention to the youth and beauty of the victims.

But there's nothing pretty, romantic or even mysterious about the situation in Ciudad Juárez, where at least 464 women have been murdered since 1993, according to the Mexico City-based newspaper La Jornada.

Many of the women have been young workers in the border city's maquiladoras, factories famous for their abusive working conditions. Many have been sexually assaulted before being murdered. A few arrests have been made, but at least one investigation has shown that police and government officials are involved in the violence. At the very least, the response of the authorities has been inadequate.

While news reports have often responded with superficial dramatizations, Caridad Svich's 2004 play IPHIGENIA CRASH LAND FALLS ON THE NEON SHELL THAT WAS ONCE HER HEART (a rave fable) dramatizes sexual violence in order to make a point. The play is set in an unnamed Latin American city where a violent general is plotting to sacrifice his daughter (IPHIGENIA), believing her death will save his political career. IPHIGENIA is a multimedia and multi-sensory experience replete with gender-bending, sexual imagery, absurdism, confusion, and Greek inevitability. It's an acid trip, and it's meant to saturate and provoke. But I'd like to highlight one aspect of the play that I found fascinating: the playwright's decision to cast Juárez's dead girls as men.

The imagery of pink crosses with women's names written on them and references to the "dead factory girls" connect the play's setting to Juárez. But the murdered women—who Svich calls fresa or "strawberry" girls, a term that can mean rich or snobby in Mexican slang—are cast as men in drag. The decision to cast the "dead girls" as men messes with the image of the young, beautiful, dead female body. In at least one version of the play, the fresa girls are cast in overdone doll makeup, wearing clothes that are too small. Such imagery satirizes the over-emphasis on female bodies in reports about sexual violence. Dressing male bodies up as "fresa girls" dramatizes the process of presenting death as beautiful or romantic. But Svich takes it a step further, challenging the privileged tendency to romanticize feminicidio. At one point, the wealthy and privileged general's daughter, who is dancing her way to a rave in order to escape her own inevitable murder, yearns to be a fresa girl—a victim of sexual violence and murder:

IPHIGENIA: I want to be just like you, girls.
FRESA GIRL 3: Like us?
IPHIGENIA: Names on a wall. Written by lovers who caress me.
FRESA GIRL 3: Caress us?
IPHIGENIA: You are beautiful girls.

Her naivete about the dead girls, murdered brutally by "lovers" outside dance clubs, indicts the naive reader or viewer. There is nothing beautiful about a dead body—even a young, female one—even one found outside a dance club.

Svich's strategic casting decision messes with canonical conventions of victimhood and confronts the idea that beautiful women somehow deserve to be raped—or that raping or killing a beautiful woman is either more or less violent than killing a less attractive *(Or less feminine)* victim. The casting of men in drag as "girls" also draws attention to violence against transgender and transsexual people and makes the point that sexual violence is not just a girl's problem. Despite attempts by the play's protagonist to dress up murder with drama, drugs and dancing, there is nothing romantic about this death—or its inescapability.

Amy Littlefield is a Providence-based journalist and an editor at the global feminist blog Gender Across Borders (www.genderacrossborders.com), where this article was originally published as part of its Theatre Rape series on January 6, 2010.

Juarez's Dead Girls: de-romanticizing feminicidio copyright 2010 by Amy Littlefield.

IPHIGENIA CRASH LAND FALLS ON THE NEON SHELL THAT WAS ONCE HER HEART

The play received its world premiere at 7 Stages in Atlanta, Georgia in January 2004. The cast and creative contributors were:

IPHIGENIA .... Heather Starkel
ACHILLES/FRESA GIRL 3 (GHOST
GIRL OF JUAREZ) .... Adam Fristoe
ADOLFO/FRESA GIRL 1 (GHOST
GIRL OF JUAREZ)/VIRTUAL MC/
SOLDIER X/GENERAL'S ASS .... Ismail Ibn Conner
CAMILA/VIOLETA IMPERIAL/
HERMAPHRODITE PRINCE .... Kristi Casey
ORESTES/FRESA GIRL 2 (GHOST
GIRL OF JUAREZ) /NEWS ANCHOR/
VIRGIN PUTA .... Justin Welborn

Director .... Melissa Foulger
Scenic design .... Ashlee A White
Costume, makeup & tattoo design .... Emily Gill
Lighting design .... Rich Dunham
Sound design .... Brian Ginn
Video design .... Sabina Maja Angel
Live action video .... Heidi S Howard
Properties design .... Patrick Campbell
Dramaturg .... Steven Yockey

CHARACTERS

IPHIGENIA, *a spinning girl of privileged means, she's used to being in the public eye, she's breaking down*

ACHILLES, *a transgendered glam rock star, beautiful and damaged (On video and live); Also (may) play* FRESA GIRL 3, GHOST GIRL OF CIUDAD JUAREZ, CHORUS.*

ADOLFO, IPHIGENIA'S *father, a contained and ambitious general (On video and live); Also plays:* VIRTUAL M C, *an obscene, liquid, techno-trip-hop vision (On video);*

GENERAL'S ASS, *a mask from the satyr play, part commedia role, part Burroughs-like dream;* SOLDIER X, *a mercenary, who has no passion left; and* FRESA GIRL 1, GHOST GIRL OF CIUDAD JUAREZ, CHORUS.

CAMILA, IPHIGENIA'S *mother, a narcotized prop wife possessed of a fierce hauteur (On video and live); Also plays:* VIOLETA IMPERIAL, *an ageless apparition, a messenger and prophet, earth-bound; and* HERMAPHRODITE PRINCE, *a mask from the satyr play, a little lost and seriously messed up.*

ORESTES, IPHIGENIA'S *baby brother, an addicted, spewing child with an adult voice (On video); also plays:* NEWS ANCHOR, *a plastic icon on the T V (On video and live);*

VIRGIN PUTA, *a mask from the satyr play, who is* IPHIGENIA'S *other twin.* GLASS-EYED MAN *(On video),* A SPECTER; *and* FRESA GIRL 2, GHOST GIRL OF CIUDAD JUAREZ, CHORUS.

Time: The present. An unnamed country in the Americas during a time of unrest.

Setting: The frame of an aircraft hangar.

Dust, dirt, and a stained party dress nailed to a battered wall. Oddly dyed carnations on the ground. The wall is jagged and impossibly high. A bank of surveillance cameras to one side: the silent, red eye.

Production & script notes: There are Spanish words and phrases incorporated in the text, which are either translated directly by a character or can be determined from context. No "Hispanic" accents should be used.

Live feed, pre-recorded video, photo stills, and projections are all part of the visual landscape of this play. Lo-tech and high-tech approaches are equally encouraged, depending on production resources.

Interactive, immersive staging is encouraged.

Doubling and tripling of roles suggested by author is preferred, for dramaturgical reasons, but other doubling options may be explored, depending on needs of production.

Melodies to original songs may be obtained by contacting the author, or the author's lyrics may be re-set by another composer.

The FRESA GIRLS *should be preferably played by men. If* ACHILLES *is not doubled, then* FRESA GIRL 3 *should be played by an additional actor.*

(As the music lightens up, the voice of the VIRTUAL M C *is heard.)*

VIRTUAL M C: Listen up, children,
or you will lose your way in this neo-psychedelic
maze.
There are rules here, you see.
Even in this grand party
of electro-tragic proportions
We have to submit to authority.
Are you willing to submit yourself to me?
Say you will, say you will, lovers and freaks,
Cause if you don't, you'll never please me,
and I like to be pleased;
Don't we all like pleasure in this regulated state of
supreme ecstasy?
Okay, okay, sluts, so this is what you do,
this is what I need:
If you want to find your way out,
there's the one you came in,
and the way opposite,
just like Orpheus and pinche Eurydice;
If you got a call waiting,
a beep beep on your beep beep mobile ringing the
latest tone from the acid police,
Shut that phone off, and shut it good.
Vibrate in the boudoir of your dreams.
And if you like me,
if you really, really give your head up
for this baby border tragedy
then come on back, swing on by,

tell your friends that the rave
keeps spinning…
A little pseudo amyl nitrate
and we're ripped fine to the bone
In this plastic synthetic hard-core fantasy
we call a new century.
But hey, sluts, at the end of a crap-ass day
there's nothing sweeter
than the feel of my virtual tongue
on your scarred knees.

Prologue

(In the distance is heard the chorus to Christoph Gluck's opera "Iphigenia in Aulis" [1774]. It is remixed to a techno beat. In the background, an image is projected on screen: IPHIGENIA, in a pink Chanel outfit, sits next to ADOLFO in a military coat.)

(In the foreground, live, ADOLFO and CAMILA sit ready for a press photograph. IPHIGENIA is at their side. She wears a double of the pink Chanel outfit in the video image.)

ADOLFO: There once was a young woman who lived in a small house by the sea, and the man who loved her.

(In the foreground, live, ADOLFO kisses IPHIGENIA on the lips.)

(In the background, image on the screen: slowly, IPHIGENIA's outfit begins to peel off her body and her skin begins to burn, while ADOLFO continues sitting, his body warm inside his coat.)

ADOLFO: He loved her so much that he would do anything for her.

(In the foreground, live, ADOLFO kisses IPHIGENIA on the lips again.)

ADOLFO: This man was her father. He was a general. He had lived with fame at his side all his life. He envied others.
He even envied his daughter from time to time.

(In the background, image on the screen: A GLASS-EYED MAN *with a cane in hand, a cane with a snake's head as its scepter, looks at* ADOLFO *and* IPHIGENIA *in flames.)*

ADOLFO: The father could tell his daughter was not happy living in the small house,
which held her day and night.

He could see that the low ceiling
hurt her head,
And her feet couldn't move without touching the edge of the front door.
He liked looking at her.
He liked having her in the house
for safe-keeping.

(The cry of baby ORESTES *is heard.)*

ADOLFO: But he would catch her looking out.
Out the window of the small house,
and the garden,
out toward the sea.

(In the foreground, live, IPHIGENIA *looks out, away from her father, who holds her by the hand.)*

ADOLFO: "Dear, sweet Iphigenia," the father would think.

(Title card on screen: "How much for her flesh?")

(Image on screen: the GLASS-EYED MAN *looks at the burning woman who was once* IPHIGENIA, *and at the warm man who is* ADOLFO. *The* GLASS-EYED MAN's *stare fills the screen.)*

(In the foreground, live, IPHIGENIA's *eyes are drawn to those of the* GLASS-EYED MAN *on the screen.)*

(Title card: "How much for her skin?")

ADOLFO: The young woman suffered from vanity.
But she never told her father.

(In the background, image: IPHIGENIA's *face is reflected in the eyes of the* GLASS-EYED MAN.*)*

ADOLFO: Iphigenia never told her father anything, despite his love for her.
And her father thought of nothing,
nothing at all.

(In the foreground, live, ADOLFO, CAMILA, *and* IPHIGENIA *are caught in the camera's flash, in tight, frozen smiles, as their photo is taken.)*

(In the background, image fills the screen: flames and a pink outfit ash.)

(In the distance, the chorus to Gluck's opera remixed to a techno beat fades.)

(In the background, only the press photo can be seen on the screen.)

PART ONE

IPHIGENIA'S FLIGHT (from the City)

(The voice of the VIRTUAL M C *is heard calling out in the darkness:)*

VIRTUAL M C: *(Voiceover)* The next, the next sound that you hear... the next sound you hear will be...

(Ambient trance music fades up.)

(In the background on a screen, a T V NEWS ANCHOR *sits behind a desk. He is "on the air.")*

NEWS ANCHOR: It is estimated that
one thousand one hundred and ten people have dis dis
disappeared today
In this land of guerrilleros
and other corporate revolutionaries.
General Adolfo will not confirm
the disappearances,
But will say that all citizens must vote for him in this
week's elections,
Which already threaten
his current standing in office,
as the opposition is starting to gain ground.
The general will need a miracle
to stay in office.

(In the foreground, live, in a garden, IPHIGENIA *is revealed in light: a blindfold over her eyes, and a branch in her hand. She wears a designer dress. There is a piñata over her,*

dangling from the air. The piñata is of a large frog, with a long, relentless tongue.)

NEWS ANCHOR: But if some great personal tragedy
were to befall him,
it is possible the country
would embrace him again.
No one can resist the tug of the human heart.
One senseless death, of a rich girl
and we will be united in grief,
sorrow, and peace.
Do you hear me, Iphigenia?

(IPHIGENIA turns slightly toward the screen.)

NEWS ANCHOR: Do you hear me?

IPHIGENIA: Iphigenia was born
centuries upon centuries ago.
I have watched her grow up,
only to see her die over and over,
story upon story.
I have lived inside her skin
Which has been rearranged
So that she will always remain a young girl
With delicate wrists and tender breasts.
And I have kept silent.
I have done my father's doing,
I have honored my mother's way.
I have let myself be adored
by the far-away gaze
Of a crowd who wants
to get a look at the girl,
a good look at the girl,
Whom fortune has blessed.
And now on this day of saints,
All I want is to be free of Iphigenia,
To be free of her certain fate.

(The specter of CAMILA, IPHIGENIA'*s mother, is glimpsed through the garden, and through the camera's surveillant eye. She shout-sings:)*

CAMILA: Iphigenia! Iphigenia! Where are you, daughter?

(In the background, on the screen, the T V NEWS ANCHOR *looks on.)*

(Behind him a blur of fragments of newscasts real and imagined swirls: a mix of atrocities and shiny products ready for mass consumption.)

NEWS ANCHOR: In the city today, Iphigenia, the general's daughter,
had a birthday. It was a private affair.
Sources will not say what she was given,
but it is estimated that there were a lot of
presents, many of them from Cartier.

(In the foreground, IPHIGENIA *strikes the piñata. She takes off the blindfold.)*

(The piñata tips for a moment, then releases a shower of dead black birds and dried black petals. Freeze)

(Light splits IPHIGENIA *into harsh angles.)*

NEWS ANCHOR:
Some say this will be Iphigenia's last birthday,
this could not be confirmed.
Nothing can be confirmed these days.
But one thing is certain:
it will only be a matter of time before death will find
our beloved girl.
It's all a matter of time down here,
in the "ass of the continent,"
Called such
by great military and diplomatic entities
who have never lost the fever

of their ambition,
Before death finds us all.

Do you hear me, Iphigenia? Do you hear me?

(The specter of CAMILA *re-appears through the garden.)*

CAMILA: Iphigenia! Iphigenia! Where are you going?

IPHIGENIA: I'm going
to the northernmost point of the city.
I'm going to shake loose the bad luck piñata
that has rained down on my head
black birds and black wings.
I'm going to dance
in the safe of an aircraft hangar
that's been turned into a ballroom.

(In the near distance, ACHILLES *is heard singing a vocal intro line from* The Deluge.*)*

ACHILLES: *(Sings)* War is over,
the gods are over,
everything,
everything is over...

IPHIGENIA: And I'm going to let
my body reign
over the ragged people with their pale gleam.

(Ambient trance music grows louder, as ACHILLES' *vocal line repeats and fades into the mix.)*

IPHIGENIA: I'm going to ooh, and aah.
I'm going to let my body be.

And stop, stop being the general's daughter
who lives in a walled-up garden
by the light of the police.

(The specter of CAMILA *re-appears. She is narcotized, half-asleep.)*

CAMILA: Iphigenia! Iphigenia! Where are you,
daughter?

IPHIGENIA: Iphigenia
is spun out onto a dark street.
Fragments of words
fall upon her as she tries to forget who she is ....
Dear gods, let me be anyone but Iphigenia.

Erase my memory, escape my death.
Only let me spin, oh gods, let me spin,
for what I seek is an angel's rest.

(The specter of a heavily narcotized CAMILA *fades through the surveillant eyes.)*

(She is a blurred image reduced to a tight close-up of soft teeth.)

CAMILA: Iphigenia...

IPHIGENIA: Iphigenia
sends herself into a phantasmagoric orbit:
a wasteland of factories and blood-red tracks.
She is nearing
the northernmost edge of the continent.

*(*CAMILA *disappears through the distorted lens of the camera, as does the* T V NEWS ANCHOR's *face from the screen.)*

(The red eye remains, occasionally blinking.)

IPHIGENIA: There is a cross
painted on a factory wall,
a large pink cross
painted over a woman's scrawled name.

(Light catches a pink cross that is painted on a factory wall's façade.)

IPHIGENIA: I look to it for comfort. *(She reads the name written on the wall. Sings)* Adina...

*(*IPHIGENIA *tries to touch the cross, which fades at her touch.)*

(Light catches another pink cross, another name.)

IPHIGENIA: *(Sings)* Natacha…

(IPHIGENIA *tries to touch the cross. It fades.*)

IPHIGENIA: Who are these girls?

(*Out of a pale neon strip,* VIOLETA IMPERIAL *appears. She is a prematurely aged woman. She pushes a small cart filled with half-cooked chicken pieces.*)

VIOLETA IMPERIAL: Girls
in newly sewn dresses. I see them.
Not like you. I can see you're different.
That's a nice dress. You buy it?
I make dresses. Cheap.
You want me to make you a dress?
I can make it right now.
I got needle and thread. See?
What kind of dress do you want, girl?
With ruffles? Cut on the seam?
Come. I make it for you.

IPHIGENIA: No.

VIOLETA IMPERIAL: Why not?
You don't like Violeta?
You don't like Violeta Imperial?
Have a piece of chicken. I got legs and wings. For
running, and flying, girl.

IPHIGENIA: I'm not hungry.

VIOLETA IMPERIAL: The aircraft hangar
is a bit further on. You'll need your strength.

IPHIGENIA: How'd you know where I was headed?

VIOLETA IMPERIAL: You're all in shadow, girl. I can
barely see you. …Hey, aren't you—?

IPHIGENIA: No.

VIOLETA IMPERIAL: Yes, you are.
You've the same face.
You're the asshole's daughter.

IPHIGENIA: My father's not an ass—

VIOLETA IMPERIAL: Take a good look. Take a look at
Violeta Imperial. *(She opens jacket to reveal a map of
scars on her body. The map of scars is also reflected in a
photographic image on the screen.)* This is your father's
doing.

IPHIGENIA: He wouldn't...

VIOLETA IMPERIAL: His men
took me into a room
and cut me open with a blade.
You hear screams?
In the dry streets
convulsing with electric signs?
Those are the screams of the innocent,
the tortured, the disappeared
that find themselves in a potter's field.

IPHIGENIA: You're not in a potter's field.

VIOLETA IMPERIAL: Some are left.
We're reminders.
A walking warning for others
who might wish to speak up against anything,
or simply live in peace.

IPHIGENIA: What did you do?

VIOLETA IMPERIAL: Nothing.

IPHIGENIA: What do you mean?

VIOLETA IMPERIAL: I was taken
into a cold room of a quiet house
made of loose cinder block
and cut open for nothing.
For kissing a girl. "Pata," they called me.
"We'll give you pata," they said
as they cut through my flesh.
I prayed to Eleggua,
the god who opens all doors,

and leads all ways.
the god who stands at the cross-roads
with his conch shell eyes
staring in the light.
You pray to him, girl?

IPHIGENIA: To Eleggua?

VIOLETA IMPERIAL: You should pray to him. I prayed.
"Prayer to Eleggua"
(Sings) Mi Dios, mi salvador, mi Eleggua.
Tell me what to do.
Tell me what to do.
And I will.
(Spoken) And he said "Close your eyes."
I fainted and let them cut me,
as I dreamed about the girl I kissed,
The sweet girl with brown eyes
and a ruthless tongue
who worked for the police,
the sweet girl who betrayed me.

IPHIGENIA: I can have her reported. I can ask my
father—

VIOLETA IMPERIAL: She's dead.
I woke up in a field at the edge of the city with her
body next to me.
They had made a hole in her throat,
and had pulled her tongue out
through the hole.
She was to be my reminder.
I don't get much kissed now.
Not with this body stitched up
by an errant doctor's hands.
Needle, thread and a splash of violet water. That's
what I got.
Violeta Imperial, Royal Violet water.
Hence my name.

You want a piece of chicken?
I got legs and wings.

IPHIGENIA: If my father knew-

VIOLETA IMPERIAL: We all love our fathers. It's a
daughter's curse.
But ask him what he's done.
And what you do by carrying his name.

IPHIGENIA: I am not my father's daughter.

VIOLETA IMPERIAL: You're going to be a bastard now?

IPHIGENIA: Those men that took you and—they will be
punished.

I will see to it. I will do whatever I can—

VIOLETA IMPERIAL: What are you going to do,
Iphigenia, with your midnight lipstick and designer
sheen?

IPHIGENIA: I was kidnapped last year.
I was taken from my bed,
stuffed inside a sack, and tossed into a jeep.
I remember my nose bleeding.
There was the smell of honeysuckle in the air.

I was taken out of the car
and tossed onto a hard floor.
I could feel the bruises
forming themselves on my skin.
I kept still in the darkness of the sack.

VIOLETA IMPERIAL: In stillness lies virtue.

IPHIGENIA: You believe that?

VIOLETA IMPERIAL: It's a saying.

IPHIGENIA: There were voices in another room. Loud
voices, and boots.
I could hear a song on the radio.

(VIOLETA IMPERIAL *begins to sing softly, underscoring.*)

"La Morna"

VIOLETA IMPERIAL: *(Sings)* All the young girls
die in my arms
die like wounded birds
strangled by the palms.

IPHIGENIA: *(Continuing)* A torch song,
the kind of song my mother sings
alone in her room at night
with the trace of vodka on her lips.
The door to the room opened.
A young man's voice said "Wake up, puta."
When I opened my eyes,
I felt strong hands poking at me. I screamed.
The young man said
"Shh. Your father's sending the money."
And he pulled from deep inside
his pants pocket some twine,
and tied my hands together,
and he took a thin strip of cloth
from inside another pocket,
and he gagged me.

(Sings softly) All the silent girls
scream in the night
letting their tongues fall
upon the broken moonlight.

IPHIGENIA: He pulled me
into another room
and flashed a camera in my eyes.
"This is for the papers," he said.
"They'll pay for a picture of you."

(Shift to the screen: T V NEWS ANCHOR *is standing against
a backdrop of a field dotted with palms. Sporadic gunfire.)*

NEWS ANCHOR: General Adolfo is trying to negotiate
with the drug cartel
To end its operation Project Zero

Which is making all the rich flee the country
in fear that their sons and daughters will be taken
away and held for ransom
There is no greater fear than the fear
of losing prominent investors
in what would be the largest growth
of the multinational dollar
in this country's history,
Either that
or having a loved one's ear sent in the mail.
(Through the screen) You hear that, Iphigenia?

IPHIGENIA: *(To the screen)* What?

NEWS ANCHOR: Nobody misses you.

(Fade on the screen. Back to...)

IPHIGENIA: A car pulled up.
My father's secretary was let in.
He carried an envelope in his hands.
It was stuffed with dollar bills.
I was quickly untied.
There were cuts on my arms and wrists
from the twine,
and piss down my legs.
The young man took me by the arm
and dragged me over to my father's secretary.
"Don't worry. She's still a virgin, cabron,"
The next day, my picture was in the papers—
The photo the young man had taken of me sitting on
the stool:
tied, gagged, and hungry.

(Front page news photo of tied-and-gagged IPHIGENIA *is
reflected on the screen.)*

IPHIGENIA: My father refused to recognize me.
"The papers will print anything," he said,
"My daughter, my dear, sweet Iphigenia, never went
through this."

I looked at my father with the memory
of the young man's hands on me.
"Father, why won't you hold me?"

VIOLETA IMPERIAL: They might as well have killed you
up there in the country.

(Photo fades on the screen.)

IPHIGENIA: What?

VIOLETA IMPERIAL: You can't do anything. You're at the
mercy of your father. Like me. Like a piece of chicken.
Want a taste?

IPHIGENIA: Here,
and into the trash with you,
remnant of the mutant underclass.

(IPHIGENIA *throws dollar bills at* VIOLETA IMPERIAL *and
starts to walk away.)*

VIOLETA IMPERIAL: I'm only speaking the truth.

IPHIGENIA: Which truth is that?
To think I almost believed you when you said all that
about being cut up by my father's men...

VIOLETA IMPERIAL: I've the scars...

IPHIGENIA: Put there by someone else.

VIOLETA IMPERIAL: What are you saying?

IPHIGENIA: I'm at no one's mercy, least of all my father.

VIOLETA IMPERIAL: You're blind, Iphigenia.

IPHIGENIA: I'd rather be blind
than a walking corpse.

VIOLETA IMPERIAL: You're your father's daughter, after
all.

IPHIGENIA: Shut up.

VIOLETA IMPERIAL: Cruelty is in your blood. Thanks to you this city will be smashed, and every soul will be uprooted from their homes.

IPHIGENIA: I gave you money.
I don't want to hear anything else.
I hear things all the time: voices, screams…
I sit in my garden
and cover my ears while my brother cries,
because he needs his fix,
he needs coca to keep him alive.
He's not even a year old
and he's already a junkie.
Look at my tits. Go on. Touch. Pata.

VIOLETA IMPERIAL: Don't.

IPHIGENIA: I want you to. I want your hands on me. Squeeze them. Go on. Feel my tits.

VIOLETA IMPERIAL: You mock me.

IPHIGENIA: I mock myself. I breast-feed my own brother. …Keep your hands.

VIOLETA IMPERIAL: No.

IPHIGENIA: I disgust you?

VIOLETA IMPERIAL: There is no place for tenderness in my life.

IPHIGENIA: I don't know what tenderness is. I look for it. All the time.
I close my eyes and pretend it exists.
And then I think of those men, of how I was taken, of how my father…

VIOLETA IMPERIAL: Iphigenia, where are you going?

IPHIGENIA: To the northernmost edge.

VIOLETA IMPERIAL: It's better for young girls not to be seen. Come, Iphigenia.

IPHIGENIA: Take the money, Violeta.
Devastate yourself for the promise
of a blessed touch from this god-less girl...

VIOLETA IMPERIAL: The chicken is good, Iphigenia. Eat.

IPHIGENIA: Do not follow me.

(VIOLETA IMPERIAL *picks up the money, and recedes into
the shadows.* IPHIGENIA *burns in the evening's acid glow.*)

IPHIGENIA: The aircraft hangar
is minutes away. I can see it from here,
from the dust and gravel road
that ruins the soles of my Gucci shoes.
I can hear the unrelenting pulse of music made to un-
still the heart.

(*In the distance,* ACHILLES *is heard singing from the chorus
of* The Deluge.)

ACHILLES: (*Sings*) And all the pretty girls
dance in the deluge.
All the pretty girls...

IPHIGENIA: Aah...
the crimson lights and purple strobe
will soothe me,
Will make this birthday more than
just a creeping, convulsive treachery
Played on me by gods
unwilling to grant me peace.

(*Light catches another pink cross, another name on a factory
wall's façade.*)

IPHIGENIA: Another pink cross, another name, and...
I am bathed in the most heavenly...
(*Sings*) Yvonne...

(*Three* FRESA GIRLS *emanate from the factory walls. On
their foreheads, metallic crescents are painted. Their club*

dresses are slightly stained. They have "anime" eyes, and shiny red lips.)

FRESA GIRL 1: *(Appears)* Yvonne? That's me.

IPHIGENIA: *(Sings)* Dulce…Magaly…Luz…

FRESA GIRL 2: *(Appears)* Luz? I'm Luz.

IPHIGENIA: *(Sings)* Aminta…Gladis…Yoli…

FRESA GIRL 3: *(Appears)* Hey. They finally spelled my name right. Yoli. With an "I" at the end, not a "y," like all the bastards think.

IPHIGENIA: Names upon names
Foreign to my tongue
I move them around in my mouth
As I run my hands across the smooth surface of these factory walls

FRESA GIRL 1: Is that where we are? I haven't been near the maquiladora in a long time.

FRESA GIRL 2: The last thing I want is to be near a sewing machine.

FRESA GIRL 3: We're here because of her.

FRESA GIRL 1: Who?

FRESA GIRL 3: Iphigenia.

FRESA GIRL 1 & 2: That bitch.

FRESA GIRL 2: She's been nipped and tucked since the day she was born.

IPHIGENIA: *(Sings)* Maria…Clotilde…Azul…

FRESA GIRL 1: Azul's gone, too?

IPHIGENIA: I feel these girls' hands on me. I feel myself pulled…

Oh, their touch warms my skin…

FRESA GIRL 1: She must think we're living.

FRESA GIRL 3: With our throats cut?

FRESA GIRL 2: *(To* IPHIGENIA*)* Hey girl, take a look at my jagged necklace.

FRESA GIRL 3: *(To* IPHIGENIA*)* Take a good look, because your blood will be let soon.

IPHIGENIA: Everything is alive here. Everything I'd ever want...

FRESA GIRL 1: Oh. She doesn't know about us.

FRESA GIRL 2: What?

FRESA GIRL 1: The fresa girls.

FRESA GIRL 3: The ripe girls,
like strawberries, who come from the deep country to work in the factories.

FRESA GIRL 2: Who spend twelve hours a day at a sewing machine.

FRESA GIRL 1: Come time to get paid

FRESA GIRL 3: Mere dollars a week

ALL FRESA GIRLS: We'd go out all night

FRESA GIRL 1: To remind ourselves

FRESA GIRL 3: What a bit of tenderness

FRESA GIRL 2: What a bit of
candy limbs and tainted love can...

ALL FRESA GIRLS: Do
to wreck
a body.

IPHIGENIA: I could be one of these girls. Who says I have to be Iphigenia?

FRESA GIRL 1: She really doesn't know about us.

FRESA GIRL 2: The shit girls of Juarez.

FRESA GIRL 3: Who find themselves dead.

FRESA GIRL 2: Killed by anonymous hands.

FRESA GIRL 1: Outside the clubs, bodies violated and slashed on the dirt-gravel fields.

FRESA GIRL 3: And no one knows…anything about las chicas de Juarez.
(To IPHIGENIA*)* Because who is going to lift a hand to save a fresa girl?

IPHIGENIA: *(Sings)* Nesha…Mora…Doris…

(The stage becomes filled with pink crosses and scrawls of women's names floating in space in a montage which frames IPHIGENIA *as she moves, transported.)*

FRESA GIRL 2: Let's scare her. Let's show her our wounds.

FRESA GIRL 1: No. She's too happy.

FRESA GIRL 2: Bitch. Look at that dress.

FRESA GIRL 3: Look at her swirl.

FRESA GIRL 2: It's a Chanel.

IPHIGENIA: The names of all these girls enter my brain. I take them on, and undulate.
Oh. I am losing myself.

(IPHIGENIA spins among the crosses.)

FRESA GIRL 3: I remember dancing.

FRESA GIRL 1: Yeah?

FRESA GIRL 3: Like she's doing now.

FRESA GIRL 1: Remind me.

FRESA GIRL 3: I remember…hips, and torso…

FRESA GIRL 2: I remember arms. Lots of arms. And feet.

IPHIGENIA: I am losing every part of me, and I'm all right.

FRESA GIRL 2: She's doing it all wrong.

FRESA GIRL 1: She doesn't know the moves. What can she know
stuck in a garden all day?

FRESA GIRL 3: I like the way she dances.

FRESA GIRL 2: It's like she's stuck inside herself.

FRESA GIRL 3: Sexy-weird.

IPHIGENIA: I want to be just like you, girls.

FRESA GIRL 3: Like us?

IPHIGENIA: Names on a wall
Written by lovers who caress me.

FRESA GIRL 3: Caress us?

IPHIGENIA: You are beautiful girls.

FRESA GIRL 1: Hey, Iphigenia. Take us to the club, will you?

IPHIGENIA: To the club?

FRESA GIRL 1: You can get us in, can't you?

IPHIGENIA: I can get anyone in.

FRESA GIRL 1: Take us, then.

FRESA GIRL 3: And we will wear our hair in pillows.

FRESA GIRL 2: And our jackets square.

FRESA GIRL 1: And we'll go among the living again.

IPHIGENIA: Among the living?

FRESA GIRL 3: Take us dancing, Iphigenia.
Take us away from the walls of these factories
Where we left our skin.

IPHIGENIA: What?

FRESA GIRLS 1 & 2: Take us.

ALL FRESA GIRLS & IPHIGENIA: Oohing and aahing into infinity.

(All FRESA GIRLS *freeze mid-dance.)*

(Burst of white noise as montage fades and music blares.)

*(*IPHIGENIA *is caught in the unending column of light of the aircraft hangar turned club. Her voice is amplified.)*

IPHIGENIA: The aircraft hangar
opens an electric wound.
Somnambulant bodies throb
under the crimson light.
Girls with cellophane chests put blue pacifiers in their
tender mouths
While Diesel shirt boys twirl and hip-shake
To a subsonic bass line.

(All FRESA GIRLS *un-freeze, and move among the throbbing mass of shadows.)*

*(*FRESA GIRL 2 *shouts over the club's noise.)*

FRESA GIRL 2: Hey. It's gotten faster.

FRESA GIRL 1: What?

FRESA GIRL 2: Everything. Look at the screen.

FRESA GIRL 3: What?

FRESA GIRL 2: The screen.

(A rapid-fire succession of images pulsates on a large screen—innocent geometric shapes, atrocities, fragments of magazine ads, jumbles of letters.)

*(*FRESA GIRL 1 *shouts.)*

FRESA GIRL 1: It's cool.

FRESA GIRL 2: What?

FRESA GIRL 3: Let's move.

*(*FRESA GIRL 3 *writhes to the sound. The other* FRESA GIRLS *join her.)*

IPHIGENIA: A thousand factory girls move as the beat consumes

The everlasting promise of sundown.
Iphigenia feels her name escape
through the pale insomnia
Of the fake Gucci, Prada, and Helmut Lang seething
around her.
"Ooh, and aah" she lets herself cry

ALL FRESA GIRLS: Ooh, and aah...

IPHIGENIA: As the cobras hiss
in the blue lounge
to one side of the wide-open hangar.
I have become invisible in this flickering light.
Lick me.

(IPHIGENIA *joins the writhing* FRESA GIRLS *midst the throbbing shadows.*)

(*On the screen, the images give sharp way to the digital image of the* VIRTUAL M C, *a floating face with an obscene mouth and liquid eyes, who speaks with the hollow, teasing, sounds of a true lounge lizard cum D J. He is the one who spins the music that keeps the writhing at maximum.*)

VIRTUAL M C: Lick her,
cries the Virtual M C,
and welcome to the end, el fin, finis!
Lick her face and rub up
against the climactic wood
of a planet about to go dust.
This is el fin, children. This is the end.
Hold onto your cojones.
We got the sound to un-still your hearts
blasting through tomorrow, hasta manana,
until the wee bleak trash can Sinatra hours
of a dim morning that will go on for days,
or until the next brutality
brings us face to face.
Lick and moan, cabrones.

Moan in the creep of this psychedelic light
Because here we do what the state says.

(On a part of the screen, the video image of ACHILLES *is found.)*

(He wears a close-fitting woman's tunic, fishnet stockings, boots, glitter lipstick, and black nails. He has a tattoo of a large tiger down one arm. Think industrial glam rock androgyne.)

(His looped vocal line "War is over, the gods are over, everything, everything is over" is barely heard underneath the thumping bass.)

VIRTUAL M C: Lift up your hands, guerrilla ballerinas
showing off your Hello Kitty straps.
It's time to smash your heads,
down those raspberry martinis,
and dream of Mars,
Because "the war is over, the gods are over, everything...,"
hijos and hijas de la gran puta, is over.
So lick the scab off those valentine lips,

(On the screen, ACHILLES offers his tongue to the
VIRTUAL M C, who places a tab of E onto it.

(Simultaneously, live, FRESA GIRL 2 *places a tab of E on* IPHIGENIA'*s tongue, mid-dance.)*

VIRTUAL M C: and give your tits and dicks up
for our very own war-bred pop myth with Day-Glo
hips that move, oh yes.

IPHIGENIA: Who's he talking about?

FRESA GIRL 2: The boy with the body. See?

VIRTUAL M C: The boy with cherry crush, crazy love,
hot pink, star red

(The image of the VIRTUAL M C *begins to disintegrate.)*

VIRTUAL M C: Lips.
Achilles.

(A piercing sound)

*(Large letters on the screen now read "Patria o Mierda."
These letters bleed into smaller letters that read "Die for
Your Country or You're Fucked".)*

*(ACHILLES is on video on all the screens. Behind him
mutated geometric shapes spin. He sings.)*

The Deluge

ACHILLES: Stoked up on the cocaine
Living with a migraine
Looking for an end to end all my days.

Strolling through the backwoods
Living on the wild glue
Taking what I can for what I pay.

Swimming with the ratas
Behind la policia
Cutting white snow on the hoods of la migra
Pulling small razors from inside mi lengua
Cutting young men en carne viva

And all the pretty girls
Dance in the deluge
All the pretty girls
Kiss...
Why don't you kiss me?

Killing for a bum rush
Off a lousy bum fuck
Putas in the corner
Begging for a blow-job

Caught in la tijera
Of a road sin pena
Spinning my brain: oh what can I, what can I...?

And all the pretty girls
Dance in the deluge
All the fresa girls
Die…

(*The* FRESA GIRLS *swoon to the image of* ACHILLES *on video on the screens. He continues singing.*)

ACHILLES: Why don't you die…?

(ACHILLES *looks at* IPHIGENIA *through the screen, and sings*)

ACHILLES: Where is your father, girl?
Where is your father?
He's left you all alone in the world.
Tell me.

(IPHIGENIA *is about to answer* ACHILLES' *image, but* ACHILLES *kisses the camera's eye, and sings:*)

ACHILLES: And all the pretty girls
Dance in the deluge
All the pretty girls
Kiss…

(ACHILLES' *image freezes on the video. Time shift. Pinspot on* IPHIGENIA, *still.*)

IPHIGENIA: Hold me. My limbs ache. I tremble. I blur.
One hundred-and-twenty beats per minute: my heart goes.

(ACHILLES' *video image fades.*)

IPHIGENIA: The fresa girls surround me with their
stained skirts, and metallic foreheads.
I move, pulse, escape.
The inside of my chest bursting.
I tease myself
into thinking no one can find me here.
And then I see you standing beside me, father
except you don't look like yourself.

You wear a smart coat and tall hair,
and you're smiling with razor teeth, father.
You place your hand over my eyes,
and whisper "Shh, angel."

(The FRESA GIRLS *hiss.)*

ALL FRESA GIRLS: Shh.

IPHIGENIA: As a knife comes into my back
and I feel myself fall a thousand feet down

ALL FRESA GIRLS: Shh.

IPHIGENIA: A thousand feet into darkness.
And you don't say anything, father.
You don't even say

ALL FRESA GIRLS: Shh.

IPHIGENIA: You just smile.
With white snow on your tongue
I am laser-lit. Suspended.
A hundred million particles of light.
Iphigenia is dying. Hold me.

(Time shift)

(Spot dims on IPHIGENIA *and the* FRESA GIRLS *as they move in an ecstatic orgy.)*

(The VIRTUAL M C *re-appears on the large screen.)*

*(*ACHILLES *image is no longer on the screen. Only geometric shapes remain where his video face and body used to be.)*

VIRTUAL M C: Well, sluts,
it looks like our kissing boy
with the pretty chemise has "disappeared,"
As our dear general Adolfo likes to say.
Isn't that right, Iphigenia?

IPHIGENIA: What?

VIRTUAL M C: Not to worry.
Our blinking eyes may catch the lipstick trace of this

divining angel
in the not-too-distant time
we have to say goodbye.
Every state has someone
to absolve them of their debts,
and well, we've got Achilles,
The glam messiah for the savagely tricked.
A little moving of those hips,
and everyone swoons on the beat.
Plunge, my million and one disgraced ones, my sorry
children
who live day to day.
Here's some ooh and aah to send you into la mala
noche of my sad dreams.

(VIRTUAL M C's *face fades.*)

IPHIGENIA: Where did they take him? Where's Achilles?

FRESA GIRL 1: I don't know. Who knows anything
around here?

FRESA GIRL 2: He's got chulo legs, eh?

FRESA GIRL 1: Yeah. And in that slip. You can see right
up his…

FRESA GIRL 2: "El chulo culo," that's what I used to call
him.

IPHIGENIA: What?

FRESA GIRL 1: The ready ass.

IPHIGENIA: Where is he?

FRESA GIRL 3: You don't want him, girl. He's inside the
screen. Stay here.

We'll keep dancing.

IPHIGENIA: He couldn't have disappeared.

FRESA GIRL 1: You want to see Achilles?

You want to kiss the twisted boy with the golden eyes?

IPHIGENIA: You know where he is?

FRESA GIRL 1: Give us the dress.

IPHIGENIA: I have to go.

FRESA GIRL 2: You're not going anywhere, Iphigenia.

(*The* FRESA GIRLS *attack* IPHIGENIA. *They tear off her dress, nylons, shoes, earrings. As they do so, they improvise a chant. Everything is captured by the camera's eye.*)

ALL FRESA GIRLS: In the land of the living, the dead will reign.

FRESA GIRL 1: Yvonne,

FRESA GIRL 2: Luz,

FRESA GIRL 3: Yoli...

FRESA GIRL 1: A litany of the dead,

FRESA GIRL 2: Of the forgotten and unforgiving
Who have been left to walk
along the fields of Juarez

FRESA GIRL 3: without graves.

(IPHIGENIA *is left wearing only a slip, as the* FRESA GIRLS *toss her clothes about and speak-sing their chant.*)

FRESA GIRL 3: Mmm. Gucci.

(FRESA GIRL 3 *exits with* IPHIGENIA's *shoes.*)

FRESA GIRL 2: Mmm. Dior.

FRESA GIRL 1: Mmm. Prada.
For her.

FRESA GIRL 2: For her

FRESA GIRL 1 & 2: Everything is for her...

(*The remaining* FRESA GIRLS *exit in the fading somnambulant beat. Silence.* IPHIGENIA *sings.*)

Prayer to Eleggua (reprise)

IPHIGENIA: *(Sings)* Mi Dios, mi salvador, mi Eleggua…
Tell me what to do.
And I won't ask for anything anymore,
But your love.

(A close-up of IPHIGENIA *on the screen.* ACHILLES *is heard singing, live.)*

"The Deluge *(reprise-variation)*"

ACHILLES: And all the pretty girls
dance in the deluge
All the pretty girls
Cry…

*(*ACHILLES *appears in performance mode. He is wearing the same tunic, boots and makeup as in his video. A pacifier hangs from his neck. He sings.)*

ACHILLES: All the pretty girls
Sing in the darkness
Letting their torsos fall
Upon the morning's light.

*(*ACHILLES *sees* IPHIGENIA. *His face is captured on the screen in a still frame as he walks away.* IPHIGENIA *follows him.)*

END OF PART ONE

PART TWO

IPHIGENIA IN BETWEEN

(A field outside the aircraft hangar. Night)

(IPHIGENIA and ACHILLES, both in their slips, are entwined. They are back-lit with neon, seen in silhouette.)

(FRESA GIRLS 1 and 2 appear. They each wear a version of the Chanel dress they tore from IPHIGENIA.)

FRESA GIRLS 1 & 2: Iphigenia moves through the killing fields
unaware of the bones in her midst.

FRESA GIRL 2: She slums
with the boy who glitters
at the furthest edge of the city.

FRESA GIRL 1: Cherry crush, crazy love, hot pink, star red:

FRESA GIRL 1 & 2: their lips bleed.

FRESA GIRL 1: Tattoo me a cross, Iphigenia.

(FRESA GIRL 1 disappears as FRESA GIRL 2 transforms into the T V NEWS ANCHOR, whilst a montage shows CAMILA and ADOLFO multiplied in the eyes of the surveillance cameras. The T V NEWS ANCHOR is outside the screen.)

(Dark Trance in the) House Mix

NEWS ANCHOR: In Chalkis or Pylos or wherever else
floods and famine...
Hundreds of thousands are killed.
There is no count.
No numbers have been released
in what is the most devastating disaster
of the century
Which changes every minute.
This is a long century
and some people like to count the days.
Though you won't find me,
ladies and gentleman,
I have been covering this story for so long
I don't get to count.
I just look for the airplane
to get me the hell out.
One more body dug up from a grave
and I will shoot them all to splinters.
Put the magazine in and let me rip.
You hear that, general? General Adolfo?

(ADOLFO *is inside the screen. The* T V NEWS ANCHOR
remains live outside the screen.)

ADOLFO: I recommend
a good plate of chicken broth
with potatoes, and yams.

NEWS ANCHOR: Is that your official statement, general?

ADOLFO: I think it's safe to say that when we move on,
there will not be a shred of evidence we were here.

NEWS ANCHOR: What about your daughter, general?

ADOLFO: My daughter?

NEWS ANCHOR: She's been missing for hours. Some say
she's been kidnapped again.
Some say you have engineered the kidnapping

yourself to have her killed,
And thus win your people's eternal sympathy, not to
mention, the election.

ADOLFO: My daughter is at home, where she always is.

NEWS ANCHOR: Like when she was taken last year,
general?

ADOLFO: No harm will ever come to my daughter. Not
from my hands.

NEWS ANCHOR: Is that what your wife says, general?

(CAMILA *is inside the screen, an oversized cocktail glass in
hand.*)

CAMILA: I hope they plaster her body all over the
papers. Hang her up, boys.
Get some bamboo and string up my Iphigenia. Screw
her 'til sundown.

ADOLFO: A general has many burdens.

(ORESTES *can be heard crying from inside the box.*)

NEWS ANCHOR: Like your son, general?

ADOLFO: My son?

NEWS ANCHOR: Orestes.

ADOLFO: He's a baby. He doesn't know about such
things.

NEWS ANCHOR: General?

ADOLFO: The name is Adolfo. Leave us in peace.

(ADOLFO *and* CAMILA *disappear inside the darkness of the
screen.*)

(T V NEWS ANCHOR, *not knowing what to do, stands for a
moment, then decides to follow them into the screen. End of
"House Mix" section.*)

(Neon rises. ACHILLES *and* IPHIGENIA *are seen. The camera
watches them.*)

ACHILLES: Slip me your dick.

IPHIGENIA: I don't have one.

ACHILLES: I thought the rich had everything.

IPHIGENIA: Don't be coarse.

ACHILLES: Does it offend you?

IPHIGENIA: Stop.

ACHILLES: You're in me. I can't.

IPHIGENIA: I like your skin.

ACHILLES: Taste it. Lick it.
Do what you will.
I am used to being devoured.
Slip me your tongue.

IPHIGENIA: I don't...

ACHILLES: You want it all, girl.
That's why you asked for the stars
to come down and screw you.
You see this? This is my hand. I'm going to stick it —

IPHIGENIA: Stop.

ACHILLES: I'm crude. I'm what you want. Lick me.
Suspend yourself in my cradle.
I am falling down
like a mutant star hungry for skin.
You are the girl-boy-thing I need.
This is another sex we're making, twin.
Kiss me.

IPHIGENIA:
...And my tongue moves through your open mouth
sinking into saliva and teeth
and all that makes you.
I watched you last night,
my eyes were transfixed.
I caught a glimmer of myself in them.

At first I didn't realize
I was looking at my eyes,
but then I looked again, and realized
They were my eyes transformed by yours, burned by
your iris.
My slip became yours,
and our legs became one.

ACHILLES: There's death here.

IPHIGENIA: Where?

ACHILLES: All around. Bones.
Bodies torn, buried in graves.
Left by men hungry for money.
You know the kind I mean.
Like those men that took you in the night…

IPHIGENIA: I don't want to think about that.

ACHILLES: Everyone knows
the girl framed in the magazine:
Buy her picture.
She'll suffer for you as you sleep.

IPHIGENIA: Did you buy a picture of me?

ACHILLES: Pleasure
comes in ways you can't even dream.
The pursuit of it blasts us all.
Rip down the wall and you will see
one hundred million atrocities
Perpetuated and executed
in the name of pleasure.
I've been asked to be frozen,
caught in an image on a screen.
"Just sing, convulsive angel.
Sing that line over and over.
Move those hips.
But don't make a sound, a true sound, because we will
kill you."

So I spit poison in the night. I graffiti my skin. I fuck my own celebrity.

IPHIGENIA: There are better pictures of me than the one you bought. I can show you.

ACHILLES: Zig down my spine, twin.
Let's make love on top of the dead bodies
that have been lying beneath us for centuries.
Because that's what you want—a touch of the obscene.

(The tabloid photo of IPHIGENIA, *bound and gagged, is projected onto* ACHILLES' *slip, his body.)*

IPHIGENIA: The fields disappear
in a sting of light
that bleeds colors foreign to the eyes.
Mouths eclipse each other. Consume me.

ACHILLES: Can you come straight through me? In a flash?

IPHIGENIA: I will burn you.

ACHILLES: Slow down.

IPHIGENIA: I want to kill the tabloid girl that envelopes your skin.
I want to bury her in your mouth and thighs…

ACHILLES: You move too fast, girl.

IPHIGENIA: You bought my picture when it was sold on the street.
Did you make love to me then?
Did you press the picture of me against yourself and blush
At the thought of me bound—?

ACHILLES: Sink to me.

IPHIGENIA: I will sink and get rid of every bit of me.

ACHILLES: What is your weakness? I will give it to you.

*(The tabloid photo engulfs them. FRESA GIRLS 1 & 2 appear.
They are in yet another version of the Chanel dress, which is
becoming unrecognizable now — barely a trace of its origin.)*

FRESA GIRL Iphigenia stirs inside the flesh of the boy
with the glitter lips
flaunting her sex for all to see.

FRESA GIRL 2: Where do you think you are, girl? You
don't get anything here for free.

FRESA GIRL 1: A tabloid lover
will find you on the debris river
and sink you into the junk food wrappers
Stretched past greasy fingers and salty lids itching for
sleep.

FRESA GIRL 2: Tattoo me a tiger, Iphigenia.
Just like the one Achilles has down his arm. Give me its
milk.

*(The FRESA GIRLS disappear. The tabloid photo fades in
flickering black-and-white.)*

IPHIGENIA: You are the sorriest boy
I ever met.
What's that you got in your bloodstream: nicotine,
caffeine, coke, glue?

ACHILLES: A Mars bar, some acid tabs, and E.

IPHIGENIA: All muscle.
Didn't you use to be an archer, boy?
A wing-footed archer
with limbs traced in golden armor?

ACHILLES: I used to be everything.

IPHIGENIA: A regular dream.

ACHILLES: Curl around me.

IPHIGENIA: I don't want anything but your tongue.

ACHILLES: Coax it. It will sing for you. I am easily won.

IPHIGENIA: Scar.

ACHILLES: Feel nothing but my tongue.

IPHIGENIA: Right on the eyebrow. You were cut once.

ACHILLES: I cut myself with a blade
when I was young.
I wanted to brand myself
before someone else would.
I wanted a mark on me.
Everyone is branded here.
Even those that pretend they are un-marked.
So, I cut. On the slant of my brow.
Until blood ran into my eyes.
Here. Look at it. Burn your candle on it.
It says I am a boy and girl at once.
And what I do, who I am,
is punishable by death,
or worse: endless repetition.
(Sings) War is over, the gods are over, everything,
everything is over...
(Spoken) The crowd trips and sways
for a trick of my light.
Take me into your bloodstream.

IPHIGENIA: Erase me.
(She takes a tab of acid from his tongue with a kiss.)

ACHILLES: We are night-crawling, girl.
Your heart is racing
inside the soft part of my chest
Where you hide like a drop of rain
And never cry.

*(ACHILLES and IPHIGENIA are rapt in the night air. They
are suspended in light, and sleep. Time shift)*

(Light comes up on silver clouds and jagged trees.)

*(Three masks appear between the trees, as if this were a
stage set: A VIRGIN PUTA, who sounds like IPHIGENIA, a*

HERMAPHRODITE PRINCE, *who sounds like* ACHILLES, *and the* GENERAL'S ASS, *who sounds like* ADOLFO.)

(*The* GENERAL'S ASS *carries a thin whip in his hand. This is played as a commedia piece for an imaginary audience. This is* IPHIGENIA's *nightmare hallucination.*)

VIRGIN PUTA: The Story of a Virgin Puta

HERMAPHRODITE PRINCE: The Hermaphrodite Prince

GENERAL'S ASS: And the Blessed General's Ass

GENERAL'S ASS, HERMAPHRODITE PRINCE & VIRGIN PUTA: A satyr play.

(*The "play" begins.*)

VIRGIN PUTA: You should've seen the sky. It was beaming green.
Pulse pulse…I was dancing.

GENERAL'S ASS: Slap.

VIRGIN PUTA: Oh, father, don't hurt me. I only wish to please.

GENERAL'S ASS: Don't you like my ass, daughter?

VIRGIN PUTA: I love it, but you can't walk around with it out in the open
all night.

GENERAL'S ASS: Slap.

VIRGIN PUTA: Oh, father, don't hurt me.

GENERAL'S ASS: You were made to be sacrificed, daughter. Open your legs.

VIRGIN PUTA: But how will I stand, father?

GENERAL'S ASS: You will be bent.

VIRGIN PUTA: Is that the custom, father?

GENERAL'S ASS: It is for all the virgin putas.

VIRGIN PUTA: How long will you stay in me, father?

GENERAL'S ASS: Until you've learned the truth about me.

VIRGIN PUTA: I prefer lies, father. They go down so much better.

GENERAL'S ASS: Slap.

VIRGIN PUTA: Do I offend, father?

GENERAL'S ASS: You have been made meat.

VIRGIN PUTA: I am still your daughter. Love me.

GENERAL'S ASS: You must resist me.

VIRGIN PUTA: I will.

(The HERMAPHRODITE PRINCE *dances, lost in himself, while in real time* ACHILLES *slips away un-noticed from Iphigenia's side, and disappears past the edge of the field.)*

HERMAPHRODITE PRINCE: *(Sings)* "Bathroom girl, oscillate those eyelids. Smuggle my gaze."

GENERAL'S ASS: Who sings? Tell me. Speak.

VIRGIN PUTA: It is a prince, father.

GENERAL'S ASS: This bitch?

HERMAPHRODITE PRINCE: *(Sings)*
"Silver strands of moaning flesh
will I be…"

GENERAL'S ASS: Do not dance for me.

HERMAPHRODITE PRINCE: Don't you want to watch me?

GENERAL'S ASS: What?

HERMAPHRODITE PRINCE: Make love to your daughter.

VIRGIN PUTA: Oh, father, please.

HERMAPHRODITE PRINCE: I'll be any sex you want me to be.

GENERAL'S ASS: Scratch her with your fingernails.
Suckle her, boy.

HERMAPHRODITE PRINCE: *(By rote)* Whore. Bitch.

VIRGIN PUTA: More.

HERMAPHRODITE PRINCE: Iphigenia.

VIRGIN PUTA: Don't call me that.

HERMAPHRODITE PRINCE: Isn't that your name?

GENERAL'S ASS: There are no names here. Only bodies.
Do as you are told.

(The GENERAL'S ASS *strikes the* HERMAPHRODITE PRINCE
on the ass with the whip.)

HERMAPHRODITE PRINCE: I bleed.

GENERAL'S ASS: Hands on her throat. That's right.

VIRGIN PUTA: But, father…

(The HERMAPHRODITE PRINCE *chokes the* VIRGIN PUTA.
She falls limp.)

HERMAPHRODITE PRINCE: *(Sings)* Iphigenia…

(The HERMAPHRODITE PRINCE *collapses.)*

GENERAL'S ASS: Her double.
But you've done the trick, bitch.
Now I will tell you how she should be killed.
Lead her into a quiet house off the main road.
She will follow you
if you tell her a lover waits for her.
Then close the door, blind her,
and pierce her with a knife.
She's not my daughter anymore.
She has abandoned me.

IPHIGENIA: Father?

GENERAL'S ASS: I love you so much I will do anything
for you. Anything.

IPHIGENIA: Father, hold me!

(*The mask of the* GENERAL'S ASS *spews black birds from its hole.* IPHIGENIA *screams.*)

(*The* HERMAPHRODITE PRINCE, *the* VIRGIN PUTA, *and the* GENERAL'S ASS *drop their masks to reveal* VIOLETA IMPERIAL, FRESA GIRL 2, *and* FRESA GIRL 1.)

(*End of "Satyr play."*)

IPHIGENIA: Iphigenia comes back to me. Her story is fresh upon my skin. Destroy me.

FRESA GIRL 1: What's the matter, girl? Didn't you like our show?

IPHIGENIA: Scavenge me. Wreck my heart.

FRESA GIRL 2: Who are you talking to, girl?

IPHIGENIA: Money. Do you need money?

VIOLETA IMPERIAL: What are you saying, child?

IPHIGENIA: Under my bed. I have new bills that aren't even in circulation yet.

FRESA GIRL 1: We don't want anything.

IPHIGENIA: What do you mean? Everybody wants...

VIOLETA IMPERIAL: We don't need anything, child.

FRESA GIRL 2: We disappeared a long time ago. Nobody needs anything from us.

IPHIGENIA: What are you—? Your throat...

FRESA GIRL 2: Razor. Right on the breath.

IPHIGENIA: You're dead?

FRESA GIRL 1: We're all dead.

FRESA GIRL 2: Another pink cross, another name... marked upon the fields of Juarez.

(FRESA GIRLS *1 and 2 start to walk away.*)

VIOLETA IMPERIAL: The country needs you, Iphigenia. We need a girl like you to give us hope.

IPHIGENIA: What?

(VIOLETA IMPERIAL *touches Iphigenia's forehead with the palm of her hand: a benediction.*)

VIOLETA IMPERIAL: You're dead.

(VIOLETA IMPERIAL *Imperial joins the* FRESA GIRLS. *They walk away, and disappear among the jagged trees. Time shift.* IPHIGENIA *is awake, trembling.*)

(ACHILLES *emerges from a part of the field. He is in a state of delirium. He is high.*)

Liquid Haze

ACHILLES: *(Sings)* Wake me at dawn
pierced through feeling
Re-inscribe the terror
Of the pulsing light.

IPHIGENIA: Achilles, did you know…?

Did you know we were being watched?

ACHILLES: *(Sings)* No sign,
No sign of trembling.
I have left you dry.

IPHIGENIA: Did you know that we are surrounded by ghosts?
You have tricked me.

ACHILLES: *(Sings)* Trick and sway
the boy twist.
He's got a gadget up his sleeve,
And he knows
How to use it.

IPHIGENIA: Look at me. Please.

ACHILLES: *(Sings)* I got a blue tab.
Do you wanna split it with me?

IPHIGENIA: You have poisoned me. My teeth gnash, are made raw.

ACHILLES: *(Spoken)* Where are you going?

IPHIGENIA: I want to hear the people scream.

ACHILLES: *(Speak-sings)* Lacerate me.

IPHIGENIA: I've heard screams in my sleep. Blinding shots of electricity:
into earlobes and soles of feet.
And I have closed my eyes,
and covered my ears.
I have pretended I couldn't feel anything.
I have been dreaming, Achilles:
reckless in sleep.

ACHILLES: You're with me.

IPHIGENIA: I have been trying to erase every bit of me,
so that I could make something else out of myself,
so that I could feel something with this body
that has been denied for so long.
But Iphigenia is still here, isn't she?
She still owes her country.

ACHILLES: You don't owe anybody anything.

IPHIGENIA: Where are we?

ACHILLES: In the sky.

IPHIGENIA: Every muscle in my body is trembling.

ACHILLES: The sun will be up soon.

IPHIGENIA: Everything hurts.

ACHILLES: Shh.

(FRESA GIRLS 1 *and* 2 *are heard hissing in the distance.
Their hiss is amplified and electronically distorted.)*

FRESA GIRL 1 & 2 *(V O)* : Shh.

IPHIGENIA: The girls hiss.

ACHILLES: What?

IPHIGENIA: The dead girls from the factory, from the club…

ACHILLES: You're dreaming.

IPHIGENIA: Are you going to kill me?

ACHILLES: …I'm a coward, Iphigenia.

IPHIGENIA: You were raised by centaurs. You'll do anything.

ACHILLES: I don't know what centaurs you speak of.

IPHIGENIA: Achilles, son of the sea-nymph, raised by a glorious centaur, a deceiver of men.

ACHILLES: That's in the past, isn't it?

IPHIGENIA: Do you remember? I remember things that I haven't even lived.

ACHILLES: I have erased everything.

IPHIGENIA: With acid tabs and a Mars bar?

ACHILLES: I am completely remade.

IPHIGENIA: I think I am what the past has made me.

ACHILLES: You think too much.

IPHIGENIA: …You won't let me die, then?

ACHILLES: …Lean on me, twin.

(ACHILLES *and* IPHIGENIA *embrace.*)

IPHIGENIA: Look. Your tiger has tattooed itself on my skin.

ACHILLES: You'll forget me.

IPHIGENIA: No.

ACHILLES: You'll walk into the club one night, and you'll spit at me.

IPHIGENIA: Don't.

ACHILLES: You'll grab my legs and trip me out of the screen...

IPHIGENIA: I'll do anything. Watch me.

ACHILLES: And you'll beam your novocaine teeth, and pound me,

IPHIGENIA: I will destroy every bit of your celebrity.

ACHILLES: *(Continuing)* as the Virtual M C strings me up and floats me above your reach:
(In the voice of the VIRTUAL M C*)*
"Pull a limb off the dangling boy, girls.
Shake his tree.
He won't feel anything.
His blood is soaked in E."

IPHIGENIA: There will be no one left to adore but me.

ACHILLES: And you'll pull off my arms
while I hang from the invisible hook
attached to the ceiling
And you'll parade my limbs for all to see.
Then another girl will take my legs
And you'll start to cut me.
"Let's make a flower from his flesh,"
you'll say.
And my twitching eyes will watch you
make a corpse of me.

IPHIGENIA: You curse me.

ACHILLES: Give me your body.

IPHIGENIA: My teeth are numb.

ACHILLES: Put this in your mouth.

*(*ACHILLES *puts a pacifier in* IPHIGENIA*'s mouth, as he turns her body against him.)*

(Shift to baby ORESTES, *who appears on the screen. He speaks in an adult voice, and is stoned.)*

ORESTES:
Right in my sock mouth yeah, that's what I need,
my sister dear, my sister be.
You are loud and right in my face.
Is that why you got me stoked up for?
I got coca in my brain since the day I was born.
I don't need any more coca cola, or any other yanqui
dollar, get me?
I bounce without any help from the motorcycle slaves
killing off girls on the side of the street.
You think I don't know anything?
Pink cross on a factory wall. That's me.
I'm the painter, dear. Your brother Orestes.

(IPHIGENIA *spits out the pacifier.*)

IPHIGENIA: Orestes?

ACHILLES: There's no one here but me.

ORESTES: I'm the one marking the time, day, and the
very santo espiritu moment
(*He makes the sign of the cross with his tiny hands.*)
of the fresa girls meeting their death outside the rave.
Rev, rev, rev on, sister.

(*A lid is placed over* ORESTES' *head by an anonymous hand.*)

ORESTES: We see he is inside a designer shoebox
labeled "Gucci."

(*Night bleeds into morning.*)

IPHIGENIA: What have you done to me?

ACHILLES: Shh.

IPHIGENIA: I'm bleeding.

ACHILLES: I'm sorry.

IPHIGENIA: You wanted to split me.

ACHILLES: We're one, girl.

IPHIGENIA: You're a monster.

ACHILLES: I'll be dead soon.

IPHIGENIA: What?

ACHILLES: I've had AIDS for years. It's all a matter of time...

IPHIGENIA: You're lying.

ACHILLES: Why do you think they show me every night dancing in the same image?
"He'll be delirious in a beat. Watch him. Watch him lose his mind.
He's our original rock n'roll suicide. "
I feel it sometimes. Words get botched. Everything goes slow.

IPHIGENIA: ...Kiss me.

ACHILLES: You still want me?

IPHIGENIA: I want everything.
I see myself in the sky, and I don't have this weird film on my skin.
The whole earth has been irradiated,
and I'm flying through the air
looking down on my house,
except it's not there anymore.
There's nothing, except land and a few flowers made of human bones
where my room used to be.
And my baby brother is swimming in this large pool shaped like a guitar,
like the one Elvis used to have.
And he's happy.
He's not drowning in coca anymore. He's free.
And I'm on the gulf where the sea is gray, and no one wants a piece of me,
not the newspapers, not the boys in fatigues, not even my father...

(She kisses him.)

ACHILLES: You kiss without shame.

IPHIGENIA: Will you betray me?

ACHILLES: Will you forgive me?

IPHIGENIA: …Give me your hands.

ACHILLES: What?

IPHIGENIA: You have bewitched me.

(Sun burns upon ACHILLES *and* IPHIGENIA *as he gives her his hands.)*

END OF PART TWO

PART THREE

IPHIGENIA'S RETURN:
SEVEN CUTS FROM A DREAM

one

(In the city's gleam, IPHIGENIA *is standing.)*

IPHIGENIA: Back arched. The neck pivots on tired
shoulders.
Iphigenia comes home from the dance.
The streets are empty.
Dots of houses lie low against the horizon.
Iphigenia is headed home,
but she takes her time.
She walks with the last trace of Achilles
on her skin.
Her father is far from her mind.

*(*VIOLETA IMPERIAL *appears. There is a dress over her arm.)*

VIOLETA IMPERIAL: You're going to need your strength.

IPHIGENIA: Get away from me.

VIOLETA IMPERIAL: You've a temper in the morning,
eh? Come on. Try on this dress. I made it special with
lace. You want to look good for Achilles, don't you,
child?

IPHIGENIA: For Achilles? Yes.

*(*IPHIGENIA *lets* VIOLETA IMPERIAL *place the dress on her.)*

VIOLETA IMPERIAL: I made you this dress, Iphigenia. From Queen Anne's lace.
These hands sewed night and day praying for your return, while another pink cross, another girl's name went up on the factory wall.

IPHIGENIA: Another girl was killed?

VIOLETA IMPERIAL: Where do you think I got the Queen Anne's lace?

IPHIGENIA: Take this off me.

VIOLETA IMPERIAL: It's all right, child. I washed it. This dress has been cleansed of all blood. You are safe.

IPHIGENIA: Hold me, Violeta. I'm scared.

VIOLETA IMPERIAL: I can't have anyone near me. You know that.

IPHIGENIA: No one will see.

VIOLETA IMPERIAL: You think because you're out here that no one can see?

IPHIGENIA: Hold me. Please.
I can feel the dead girl's breath inside this dress. I feel all the dead through me.

VIOLETA IMPERIAL: Girls die every day here, and no one mourns them.

IPHIGENIA: I want to mourn them, Violeta. I want to free them of their pain.
I want your scars on me.

VIOLETA IMPERIAL: Look around you, Iphigenia. There are eyes everywhere. They've seen everything. Your death will help us make some sense of it all. Our grief will finally have a place.

IPHIGENIA: I'm not dead.

VIOLETA IMPERIAL: They're selling pictures on the street.

(The screen flashes a thousand photos of IPHIGENIA's *body splayed on the field outside the club.)*

(In each photo, her eyes are either ecstatically blank, or scratched out.)

VIOLETA IMPERIAL: We need someone to mourn for, Iphigenia.
We need a girl we can look up to.

(The screen rests on a close shot of IPHIGENIA, *slightly bloodied, with the pacifier in her mouth.)*

VIOLETA IMPERIAL: This one's my favorite.
Fifty dollars for a premium shot of Iphigenia sucking on her baby blue.
Of course, I wouldn't sell it. I sell chicken. Legs and wings.
For running, and flying, see?

(The close shot of IPHIGENIA *with blank eyes is magnified now. Image upon image. Eyes, mouth, nose. Cropped shots overlaid as* VIOLETA IMPERIAL *fades into the periphery.)*

IPHIGENIA: The dress of a dead girl
sticks to her skin.
Iphigenia sees her father's eyes staring at her from behind the screen.
The centuries fade in ribbons. Father...?

*(*SOLDIER X, *a mercenary, appears.)*

SOLDIER X: Give us back your body, girl. It's never been yours to keep.

IPHIGENIA: She closes her eyes against the sky as it turns to day.
Away from her dreams. Away.

two

(SOLDIER X *and* IPHIGENIA *stand a few feet apart from each other.*)

IPHIGENIA: When will you kill me?

SOLDIER X: I'm a mercenary, Iphigenia. I kill for money, not out of rage.

IPHIGENIA: Has my father paid you yet?

SOLDIER X: Let's not discuss such things.

IPHIGENIA: Make my father pay you.
I want you to lead me into a quiet house
off the main road,
and tell me Achilles is waiting for me.
I want you to close the door, and cover my eyes and
when I ask "Why?"
I want you to pierce me with a knife.

SOLDIER X: You're growing up too fast, girl.

IPHIGENIA: I never liked childhood.

three

(IPHIGENIA *talks to* ORESTES, *who is inside the designer shoebox.*)

(ORESTES's *face is seen on the screen.*)

IPHIGENIA: I don't think you will ever grow up. You haven't grown an inch since I put you in here. You're so thin, and your fingers are so… Your eyes are spinning, Orestes.
Stop looking at me.

(IPHIGENIA *rocks the box.* ORESTES's *face contorts in restless, wide-eyed sleep on the screen. She sings.*)

Lullaby for Orestes

Marry the winged messenger
with a foot on the grave.
Here we do what my father says.
The fresa girls work in factories all day

Waiting for young men to kill them.
Dream, dream, Orestes.
Dream, dream, with blood on your mind.
Dream, dream, Orestes.
Dream my death
With your stoned eyes.

four

(CAMILA *is combing her hair.* IPHIGENIA *watches her.*)

CAMILA: Iphigenia's the eldest. My first. I'm supposed
to be proud of her.
But when I look at her, I feel hatred.
Inexplicable, for it was an easy childbirth
I had with her.
Her brother, on the other hand, was hard. They had to
cut me open.
But Iphigenia popped out in minutes,
eager to be out in the world.
She burns my fingers.
She is the fruit of Adolfo's rape of me.
Such glorious, poisonous fruit.
He married me against my will.
He smashed the head of a baby boy whose name is no
longer remembered
And stuck his cock inside me.
For the good of the country.
For the promise of a model wife at his side.
"My dear, sweet Iphigenia," Adolfo would say. "She is
the best of us."

I slap her. Across the face.
I make her take care of her baby brother, because I
know he cries all night,
and she won't be able to sleep.
I know what she wants.
She wants to touch me. Like any daughter.
Iphigenia. I will never love you.

five

(IPHIGENIA *walks like a ghost through her own house, and
out into the street, toward the light of the hangar, past
everything.*)

IPHIGENIA: It is night. I see fragments.
My mother braids her hair in the moonlight.
My brother cries from inside the box that once held my
Gucci shoes.
My father sleeps with his feet facing the window. I kiss
him for the last time.
No tears, father. Everything will be all right.
I move to the whispers
of soldiers in neon out on the street,
outside the house that holds me.
The fresa girls leave the factories
with their party dresses on.
Hey, girls. Let's go dancing.

Pulse I go in the mirror-ball. Pulse...
Spin, spin a drop of magenta green
in the open sky.
Give me a kiss, fair Achilles,
give me a deep, wet dizzy with E...
I am caught in my father's eyes.
They stare out of every camera.

(IPHIGENIA *motions to* SOLDIER X, *who appears out of the
shadows.*)

IPHIGENIA: Lead me now, soldier.
Be my blissful mercenary.
(*She offers him her arm.*)
This is how I want to be remembered:
With E on my tongue,
and the rush of love in my heart,
And the whole world spinning with my glory.
Pulse. Pulse. I go.

(SOLDIER X *takes* IPHIGENIA *in a shiver of electric light.*)

six

(*The* FRESA GIRLS *at the club are on the T V screen.*)

FRESA GIRL 1: Yeah, I saw her. She had a Chanel on.
She was looking for Achilles.
You think I look good? I've been thinking about plastic
surgery.

FRESA GIRL 2: Everybody was dancing. I couldn't see
anything. Hey. Hey. Do you like Prodigy?

FRESA GIRL 1: I could make myself into her. With the
right smile, the right teeth...I could be Iphigenia.

FRESA GIRL 3: Hey. Hey. Don't you want to talk to me?
I saw everything. Yeah.
Soldier X, the mercenary, came in through the back of
the club. She waved to him.

ALL FRESA GIRLS: What?

FRESA GIRL 3: She was no saint. I saw her. You hear
me? I saw him kill her.
I saw everything. Like I had the eyes of God. Hey.
What are you—?

(*Sound and image out on the T V. T V* NEWS ANCHOR's
face fills the screen. He is "off-camera".)

NEWS ANCHOR: No, Walter.

I do not know where the Knicks are playing tonight.
Can't you goddamn look it up? This is the information
age, for God's sake.
Everything's at the touch of a… What? What?
(He is "on the air")
In late news tonight, the general's daughter Iphigenia
is said to be dead.
I repeat, "this is a rumor,"
But sources tell us she was seen
outside an aircraft hangar
shortly before midnight
escorted by a man yet to be identified,
and she has not been seen since.
Unlike other incidents
involving the general's daughter,
reports lead us to believe
this is not a kidnapping.
Blood has been seen on the ground
at a short distance from the hangar
in a house made of cinder block.
And experts confirm
it does match Iphigenia's blood type.
I repeat "This is a rumor. This is a rumor. This is a
rumor."

*(T V NEWS ANCHOR fades as ADOLFO is seen, live. He
wears pajamas.)*

ADOLFO: She was very still. I made the sign of the cross
with my hands.
The man took out the knife.
My daughter's cry was heard but once.
When I lifted my eyes, she was gone.
There was blood everywhere.
But no sign of my Iphigenia.

*(In the background, ADOLFO is seen on video, dressed in a
military coat. He speaks to the nation.)*

ADOLFO: *(On video)* God took her.
I believe God's will has been done.
We must pray that all the fighting will stop.
We must remember Iphigenia,
and everything she did for us.
As your leader, I will do my best, in this time of great
sorrow for our family,
To live up to her precious memory.
Iphigenia is a saint.
(Live) I will be re-elected.
No one will throw a father who has just lost his
daughter out of office.

(CAMILA appears, live.)

CAMILA: A saint?

ADOLFO: Listen, Camila. The people are praying. She
escaped death.
She'll save us all.
(On video) In Iphigenia's name.
I call for our nation to be united.

CAMILA: My dear Iphigenia, where have the gods taken
you? Where are you, Iphigenia?

(ADOLFO embraces CAMILA.)

*(The sound of baby ORESTES crying in the background. Fade
on the scene)*

*(The VIRTUAL M C comes up on the screen, disembodied,
and grinning in the light.)*

VIRTUAL M C: Well, my little sluts,
it looks like our dancing daughter
has taken flight.
Angels bring her rest while we change places on a
wooden bench
and take our crystal high.
If it's not one brutality, it's another,
and the way we count the days is

by the pulse of this light.
Skip on, crashers. Shine on.
You get me, dolls?
This is about pig tails and ankle socks
and setting yourself up
for burying your heads between your knees.
There is no tomorrow, children.
There is only the night.
And we're going to live it through for eternity.

(The VIRTUAL M C*'s grin escapes the image of* ACHILLES, *live, who nevertheless seems to be ghosting a corner of the ever expanding space. He sings in performance mode.)*

My eyes to your eyes

ACHILLES: Insomnia trace my skin to you.
My eyes to your eyes,
My eyes to your eyes.

(Image projected on the screen: close-up of IPHIGENIA*'s face through a surveillance camera.)*

ACHILLES: Save the hour, sweet angel,
And I will follow.
Hold your breath, dear angel,

And I will follow.
I will follow.
Peel off my scab, restart the wound.
I will follow.
I will follow...
(He disappears into the darkness.)

seven
Iphigenia in Extasis

(A view from the camera. IPHIGENIA *remains. She is both live, and on the screen.)*

IPHIGENIA: Crash.
I am not cut, but I am bleeding.
There is black sand on my feet, but no water.
Only the sound of waves rushing.
I am standing.
I have wings.
They grow out of my shoulder blades
Out of the veil of the T V screen.
I am not cut, but I am bleeding.

Crash.
I remember falling,
Kissing
Through the garden,
To the neon lights on the street,
Splitting me into threads of skin.
Wings lift me.
I am moving.
I am at the edge of the city.
I am atop the aircraft hangar and its beams of green.
Boys, girls and a million vacant eyes.
Look at me.
I stand on the metal ledge.
Black liquid sand slipping off my skin.
The story has been told again.
A wreath has been placed upon Iphigenia's head.

Crash.
Every part of me is breaking.
But I'm all right.
Give me your hands.
Give me your hands,
Cause you're wonderful.

END OF PLAY

Afterword

Euripides' Children

"We're all kids of E…"

This is a trance tale, of death and dying, of dancing and swaying, of divination, hypnosis, religion, and ecstasy. This is a tale told from the breath of myth (or some would say, the breach of myth) through Euripides' pen through to Calderon de la Barca's *The Monster of the Gardens* (1667), Racine's *Iphigenia* (1674), and Gluck's opera (1774) to Garcia Lorca's lost manuscript to versions told again and again, and now resting in my mouth, in my body, coursing through my veins. This is an "ambient translation" (to use musician/mixer Bill Laswell's phrase) of a story that has been translated from the ancient Greek to the French to Spanish to English and back again. In every version, the same impulse seems to arise: how to rescue Iphigenia? How to keep her from sustaining the fate to which she seems destined in Aulis? How can Iphigenia escape death? The impulse drives Iphigenia herself, who is a woman trapped inside the systematic corruption of a society which will not give her a voice, a body she can call her own unless she offers that voice, that body, to the state. Iphigenia is trapped by a notion of heroism that is not even hers, but which over time she has been made to believe is noble. This is a tale about cowardice, lies, celebrity, ambition, and sacrifice. And love. Above all, love. Deep, passionate, screwed-up love…

The Ceremony of Memory

Ecstasy *(from the Greek for "being placed outside)*, a state of exaltation in which the self is transcended

Step into the warp, which is reading Euripides' text, and the feeling of being angry. His text has the force and savage, despairing wit to anger, even today in the year 2004, when we're supposed to be past all that. How could this girl accept her death, her forced destiny, so willingly? How can she love her father so much? And her country? Is this patriotism or foolishness? Or a bit of both?

Release the victim from the thread of time, and set her in a landscape of dirt, and rituals all too alive. Images are conjured up: a collage of countries: Nicaragua, Mexico, Columbia, Panama, Argentina, Cuba, Bosnia, the U K, the U S, etc. The global marketplace and all its histories in the whirling bits and bytes and bleeps that do not even let us take in one disaster before another strikes. And not even disasters but how about people's lives? Continuity. Is there time for that these days? Who remembers the "disappeared ones" in Argentina besides the mothers of the Plaza de Mayo who stand there day after day? That was in the mid-1970s. Ancient history. Who recalls the bitter fights in Nicaragua? Who opens their eyes and looks at what is truly happening in Columbia? The rush to move on to the next and next had produced a culture of people who only wish to look away, or look up: individuals addicted to release. The Western world is in a state of constant departure.

A swirl of sounds mixes in the night air as the template of rave culture plays in the background, allowing for the consumerist totems of this culture—a drug called Ecstasy; designer clothes that elaborate on infantilism, kitsch, S & M and retro hippie-ness to enact their own

mad neo-mod game; a repetitive mix of loops and
hard-driving beats that live somewhere between glam,
disco and Philip Glass — to spur feelings of departure.
Listen up. It's Brian Eno, and Kraftwerk time again.
It's about letting the body rage in the in-between stage
all night, and straight through morning. No doom and
gloom here in this nocturnal wonderland. After all,
haven't we licked AIDS? That was the 1980s and 1990s,
right?

Iphigenia lives in the walls of culture and descends to
find herself. She sets herself loose onto a world she
doesn't quite understand, filled with the memory of
knowing too well what awaits her in the unchanging
pattern of fate, and wondering what she can do to
wreck it now, if she can. Eleggua is a god in the
Santeria pantheon, in the syncretized religion that was
born in West Africa and Cuba and then made its way
to Brazil, the US and other countries. He is the god
who opens all doors, and guides the paths of those
lost. He stands at the cross-roads with conch shell eyes
and an open brain. He watches you being split in two.
If you pray to him, you will find your way. Iphigenia
begins to pray "Mi Dios, mi salvador, mi Eleggua (My
god, my saviour, my Eleggua)," because sometimes
you have to reach past sanctioned, "official" religions,
you have to reach past to something ancient to find
even a glimpse of an answer to sustain you on your
life's journey.

The prayer is set against the relenting eye of the media,
which haunts without even wanting to. It is part of the
camera's function to look, to fix the gaze, and cultures
are built around the rapt stare, which entrances its
citizens in front of the many screens which populate
our midst. Even the "disappeared ones" are haunted
through lovers' memories, enemies' worries, and the

living's constant look over the shoulder which says "will I be next?"

The prayer gives way to a mistrust of faith. The nation becomes a cadaver as Iphigenia roams outside the cage which has held her over time and centuries. The voice is made corporeal (through screams, through song) as the blindfold, which has been placed willingly and thus begging for the relinquishment of self-direction, is cast off, and the stumbling toward something which can be found through the body's own desires begins.

The Body Politic

The body who has become an object to society, which has been already violated and trashed and reconfigured, seeks a bit of tenderness. Pleasure has been killed, you see. Iphigenia wishes to rediscover pleasure, and her body. The split persona longs for some kind of integration, but the state which governs and censors bodies and dismantles them, makes it hard for her to do so.

Iphigenia encounters the first of many mirrors in a woman who is part messenger, part prophet, and part her own creation. Violeta Imperial is a victim of torture, a member of the living "disappeared," who through her invisible status in society, rendered so by the state, moves freely in the corners, alleys, and countryside selling pieces of animal bodies to those hungry enough to buy. She has been marked verbally as a pata, a "dyke," (and thus, outside prescribed sexual laws), and doubly marked physically by soldiers eager with the blade. By escaping death, she now serves to court the present and living dead who cross her path.

This traumatic mirror conjures traumatic memory from
Iphigenia, the pristine girl who has been scarred by
culture, and rape. As Clytemnestra, now called Camila,
was herself raped by Agamemnon, now called Adolfo,
the violation of the female body and its subsequent
brutalization lives in Iphigenia's skin.

"All the young girls/die in my arms/die like wounded
birds/strangled by the palms"

the song goes as it mourns for Iphigenia's forgotten
body, which she is seeking to remember, dis-member,
and put together again. The song plays as an elegy
for body all too living and already being mourned by
celebrity's addictive fix.

Memory jars, as longed-for affection is recalled. A
father much loved by his daughter will no longer touch
his child because tears must be avoided, and a new
face must be put forth to deny the old one. Guilt hides
in Adolfo's cheek, and Iphigenia, who once again,
is faced with the specter of death, throws a veil over
the mirror called Violeta Imperial, who recedes in the
shadows, but will remember her.

Vectors of Identity

Accustomed to public spectacle, the split body searches
for private space. Ecstasy transports, lifts, and carries
the soul until the heart cannot go on any longer, until
bliss is too overpowering. A bacchanal of the spirit that
melts into the brain. And it's just another day. Another
day at the factory where the fresa girls work for forty
US dollars a week in maquilas all over Latin and South
America, where offshore riches are made by giant
conglomerates (are there any other kind?) who prey
on the dreams of girls longing to rise out of poverty

and into a more "glamourous" world where certain
material things can indeed be bought for a price.

Split souls meet other split souls, and Achilles is
remade into a new shape for our times. A hero turned
inside out for another age. A body longing for death
but not able to die. His mother Thetis, the sea-nymph,
dipped him into the River Styx to make him immortal.
The waters made him immortal except for the heel by
which his mother held him. The heel bleeds now, and
keeps bleeding. He has been touched by a modern
plague. He lives with the plague taunting him with
mortality every minute. But this soldier who has
become another kind of icon, a rock star, continues
to play. In a world where the D J reigns, this rock
star heeds Buddy Holly's call to "rave on." There is
no respite for this man idolized from Homer down
through Rubens' painting *The Death of Achilles* down
through W H Auden's *The Shield of Achilles* (1955)
down through the present when his name is but a click
of a web-link away from the imagination and hey, isn't
that golden boy Brad Pitt wearing Achilles' armor in
Troy (2004)? Achilles' body has been traversed by all
zones, and is still standing. Some flesh must remain for
the eventual slaughter. A rough and tender beast in a
silver dress and fishnet stockings, in a slip and combat
boots, in perpetual transformation, slouches toward
Bethlehem to be dilated and thus, be born.

The surface of Achilles' skin is inscribed. This is
another semantic space. A symbolic contract has been
made between Achilles and society, as has one been
made between Iphigenia and society. Twin encounters
twin. Two celebrities caught in different lenses of
experience: one escapes myth's hold through drugs,
the other seeks to both claim, and escape myth, and
thus be free of its hold forever. Identities are disguised
in an effort to act against the tyranny of social roles

who have designated a body must live by certain quotations only. Altered states illuminate wounds. Paranoia, and dreams of destruction set in. The meta-hell is the body in knowing pain: refusing anesthesia even while under the spell of the drug which ravages, damages, and plays myriad tricks with the chemicals which make it up.

Root is what we're after: origin. A fire that not only burns, but hurts. As crime and violence is ever closer to us in this society, we are ever more distanced from an active and ethical relationship with the original event. Ethics fall away, and we are left in a heretical place where hell is stored in someone else's eyes.

For every act of erasure, there is an act of recuperation, or an attempt to do so. As the self becomes more and more separated, it becomes more difficult to recover what has been lost. Has Iphigenia been lost to us forever? Will acts of recovery ever grant her rest?

The tattoo moves from one body to the other. Iphigenia finds herself through someone else's sign. Her snatch meets Achilles' velvet orbs and a new sex is made, the sex of celebrity offering itself up to the heavens for absolution. This is an assault on Babylon, and the penultimate act of erasure.

Sacrifice

Iphigenia departs her body in order to find it as the fresa girls, the ghosts of girls killed by the hundreds in border towns along the Americas, dream of her caressing their wounded flesh. These ghost-girls mark the landscape. They are the dead whose deaths are not claimed: violated bodies left on roads, outside dance clubs, killed for sport, because they belong to an economic class which has no power. Pink crosses are

painted on walls and lampposts and street corners by
those who remember them, those who wish

someone to remember the dead. The fresa girls (the
ghosts of the Women of Juarez) dream of the icon that
has been given to them, the Iphigenia they wish to
possess, and whose manner they wish to appropriate,
and they wonder what's happened to the girl who
has abandoned them to seek her own pleasure. What
burden for a young woman in any station?

How can Iphigenia meet everyone's dreams and
expectations? Isn't death the perfect answer for a life
that has been continually robbed by everyone since the
day she was born?

Ecstasy, the designer drug of choice that crosses all
class boundaries, leaves the mouth dry, and teeth raw.
Everything grinds in the mouth, the gums hurt, and
a pacifier provides instant comfort, not to mention,
it makes a great fashion statement. Look at me, the
pacifier says. I'm your baby now. I'm your bit of baby
kink. Come into my mouth, pry open my lips, if you
dare. The heart races in constant acceleration, and
transcendence of a kind is found in a drug-induced
fever dream.

Achilles' mirror betrays as the immortal one begs
leave of the mortal. Iphigenia belongs to her country,
to the state, to her father and mother, to Orestes, who
still rocks in his cradle and can only hint at thoughts
of murder. She belongs to everyone but herself. She is
in the grip of myth, not of the gods, and so she must
die. A torturous rest awaits this stuttering child who in
order to drown her appetite has drowned her-self.

Death as fetish. Death as commodity. In the cadaver
state, elaborate rituals are created to play with the
dead. Tortured bodies are re-tortured and mutilated,
dis-membered, and treated as objects for YouTube

sport, and a new kind of profession emerges: the
specialist in cuts. Grotesque manifestations of damaged
psyches dot the landscape: a bizarre, irrational
"beauty" that bears no explanation in the condoned
bacchanal of the spirit.

"Mi corazon esta en llamas, mi corazon esta en flor /

Mi corazon se vuelve polvo, ante el espectro de tu
amor.

(My heart burns, my heart blooms/My heart turns to
ash before the specter of your love)

One of Achilles' songs can be heard as a show is played
in front of an imaginary crowd. There is no applause
here in this newly found place of jagged edges, only
screams. This is the earth Iphigenia must walk to find
her way home.

A cut in the membrane, and another, as Euripides
mocks the decisions of men made in the name of war,
and therefore, peace. Agamemnon lives inside his
mask, suffering but also able to contain the measure
of it to expedite his ambition, to satisfy his greed.
Clytemnestra will one day avenge the miseries inflicted
upon this fallen house, but in the mean time, cruel
vanity consumes her.

Reach down into the nothingness. Write this in blood.
Iphigenia holds a miracle in her hands.

Prophecy

As the record spins, and everyone celebrates
shamelessly in the wake of a young girl's death (what's
another young girl's death when so many fresa girls
have died, when so many are buried under lush trees
feasting on broken bones?), Iphigenia can see the city
and all its inhabitants burning. She reaches out with

her hands. She dreams of Mars. She imagines herself forever silent and cannot breathe for a moment. Then she thinks of a star. She thinks of creatures designed for amusement, to help societies get by in midst of chaos.

She is such a creature. She is the photograph in the exhibit, on the dinner-plate, immortalized and memorialized in bronze, silver, and tin. Dolls will be made in her image. Children will play with these dolls and try to look like her. Her dresses will be copied and re-sold to the highest bidder. Iphigenia's fashion will always be in vogue because to wear her clothes is to be her, isn't it? To be the heroine, the martyred heroine, is the ultimate accomplishment for many a young woman. Starve a little, hold everything in. Be flesh-less. Be invisible. Escape.

Iphigenia remembers a song once heard on the radio (was it Bowie in his Ziggy days claiming his "Rock n' Roll Suicide?" Was it Marilyn Manson? Lou Reed? My Chemical Romance?), and she smiles through the cuts on her skin, cuts made from Euripides' time on down. She smiles through everything. Her smile has been fixed for the camera. But as the song plays in her head, something true emerges, an expression not found in the stack of photographs and films and digital images and videos left behind. For Iphigenia recalls how to hold onto someone else can be wonderful.

Breath

I hold Iphigenia in my hands. She fits in my palm. Her breath moves through me.
I look in the mirror. Is that her face…?
Tremble. Blur.
I let her go.
This is the way.

CPSIA information can be obtained
at www.ICGtesting.com
Printed in the USA
LVHW010133300621
691473LV00012B/1939